MW00436606

# As a Mom
# THINKETH

# As a Mom
# THINKETH

A MOTHER'S GUIDE TO UNLIMITED WEALTH

DEL-METRI WILLIAMS

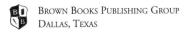

BROWN BOOKS PUBLISHING GROUP
DALLAS, TEXAS

For information, please contact Brown Books Publishing Group
16200 North Dallas Parkway, Suite 170, Dallas, Texas 75248
www.brownbooks.com
972-381-0009

ISBN 0-9729930-0-2
LCCN  2003092542
First Printing, 2003

# DEDICATION

This book is dedicated to
my wonderful husband Rudolph and
my two children Christian and Judah.

# CONTENTS

# FOREWORD

For the last two decades I have been writing, lecturing, teaching, and coaching thousands of people about the importance of establishing multiple sources of income. I have been No.1 on the *New York Times* best-seller list with two books: *Nothing Down* and *Creating Wealth,* and my newest best-sellers are *Multiple Streams of Income, Multiple Streams of Internet Income,* and *The One Minute Millionaire* with Mark Victor Hansen.

People often refer to me as America's millionaire mentor, because I have probably created more millionaires in this country than any other single person.

Del-Metri Williams is also one of my protégés, and she has made it her passion to empower mothers to make an investment in their financial future by increasing their financial literacy.

The journey towards wealth begins with your attitude. Mothers must decide that it's okay to be rich. Moms would love to have more choices in life: more time with the kids, the opportunity to send them to better schools, and more money—but they do not think these choices are available to them.

I have personally mentored numerous people and seen them reach their goal of financial freedom. After reading

*As a Mom Thinketh,* mothers will have the courage to implement wealth-building strategies because they now know they can do it . . . and because they now know they deserve it! This paradigm shift for mothers will ultimately result in greater financial freedom and more time for their families.

Prosperously yours,
Robert G. Allen,
Coauthor, *The One-Minute Millionaire*

# ACKNOWLEDGMENTS

So much goes into doing a book, which has taken me two years to complete. I would like to especially acknowledge the following:

To my husband Rudy and children Christian and Judah, thank you so much for your support. I cannot express in words the appreciation I have for giving me the freedom to pursue my passion.

To my spiritual mentors Terry and Renée Hornbuckle, your training and coaching has made it possible for me to believe I can fulfill all of my dreams and visions.

To my money mentors Robert G. Allen and Mark Victor Hansen, you have taught me so much about money. This book would not be possible without you. Thank you for generously giving your time and knowledge.

To my parents Lon and Sedalia Bynum, you always believed in me. Thank you for your lifelong support and love.

To my mother-in-love Louise Williams, you are like another mom to me. Your support is very much appreciated.

I cannot forget those from an older generation who have imparted wisdom into my life; Papa and Nana Bibbs, Dad and Mom Vaughn, and LaVoice Hornbuckle many thanks.

My deepest appreciations for those who helped make this book come together. To the staff at Brown Books, you are wonderful. Milli Brown, my publisher, your enthusiasm and commitment to this book is refreshing. I also want to thank Kathryn Grant and Alyson Alexander for your excellent work.

To all the moms featured in this book, I am grateful for your willingness to help other mothers through your stories.

And finally, to my vision partner Sara Conner, you were the first person to tell me to write. Thank you for your support; may all your dreams come true.

# INTRODUCTION

# WAITING TO INHALE

Length of days is in her right hand;
and in her left hand riches and honour.
—PROVERBS 3:16

# Mommy Myths

For generations the role of mothers has been to put everyone else first. Then at the second half of the twentieth century it was decided that mothers would take on a career and obtain all they could professionally. Out of the stay-at-home box for the first time, mothers saturated themselves in their careers and let other women rear their children. The controversy over this new development put mothers in a new bind. They now had a choice—stay at home or work—but neither option was desirable. This choice limited mothers to a role restricted by other people's definition. Motherhood was based on the perceptions of society, many of whom were not moms. As a mom, a woman was either 100 percent mommy or 100 percent careerist. As a mother, society forced women to choose sides. Each decision meant extreme sacrifices. After all, moms cannot be wealthy, have a career, and spend quality time with their children. That is what society told us and we believed it!

A woman who had worked professionally before becoming a mother could (a) stay at home, giving up the material benefits and accomplishments she had worked so hard to achieve or (b) continue working and forfeit the joys and responsibilities of parenting.

Some choice! Talk about a lose-lose situation. Motherhood began to mean, by definition, giving up on career dreams. And when sacrifices were made, moms were the ones most often making them. When a husband and a wife "agreed" that a woman would stay at home to be with the children, the woman often took the responsibility for the lowered household income. She then traded in her car for an older one, cancelled manicure appointments, and even skipped meals to save money.

And if she continued working? Oddly, expenses such as child care somehow would get deducted from mom's share of the earnings. She would still have to scrimp, as well as take on the emotional and physical toll of "abandoning" her baby. She would then assume the extra household duties that demanded at least six hours a day (more if the baby got sick) on top of her regular work shift.

## It Happened to Me

I was put in the position of choosing to stay at home or continuing my career over six years ago. My husband and I decided it was best for me to stay at home, but in my mind I constantly struggled with that decision. I felt that society offered me an all-or-nothing choice. I was not what society said a stay-at-home mom should be. For example, I chose to read *Multiple Streams of Income* rather than *What to Expect the First Year*. The truth is, I was not the mom either side thought I should be. I heard many complaints from mothers who worked outside the home. They did not spend enough time with their children. They hit a glass ceiling, or they hated their jobs. The mothers who stayed at home complained they were worn out. They needed a mommy-break. Neither side was truly happy. Each side worked so hard to live up to society's standards, they could not see the potentially fulfilling opportunities that were open to them.

When we, as mothers, conform to societal norms, we allow others to create our world. We should never let others create our world. They will always make it too small. Our culture puts mothers in a box, which limits the creative thinking that allows moms to tap into their own natural abilities to create wealth.

## The Deception

Let's face it. Too many mothers are making pharmaceutical companies rich by filling prescriptions for antidepressants and antianxiety drugs. They are so busy pleasing everyone else, they suffocate themselves. Unfortunately, many moms feel guilty if they do anything for themselves. Moms feel like they are doing the right thing when they put themselves last, while secretly resenting their actions. In the psychological world it is called dissonance. They think and feel one way, yet they behave the opposite. Moms, who have no other choice but to internalize their inner conflicts, leave the door open to stress-related illnesses.

The great debate between stay-at-home moms and working moms often presents a dichotomy to women that forces them to choose one side or the other. What about what the mom wants to do? What does a mother do who is talented in finance, but is told it is morally wrong for her to work? How about the single mother, who would like to stay home with her children, but to whom it seems financially impossible? Each side limits the mother's thinking to only two choices.

Until moms find their true passion, they will have problems with the decisions they make. Moms must change their thinking to accept who they really are, and when they look inside themselves they will find their true purpose in life. Mothers must be comfortable with the idea that they can be more than a mom. Letting others define the mother's role will inhibit her from pursuing things that refresh, reenergize, and rejuvenate her, allowing her to give more to her family.

Flight attendants instruct passengers to use the oxygen masks themselves before attempting to aid a child during an in-flight emergency. Ignoring this procedure puts both lives at risk. Similarly, one of the most tragic decisions a mother can make is to put all of her energy and passion into everyone else while she ignores herself. Many mothers agree with the statement, "I am 99 percent mom and 1 percent me."

Mothers need oxygen, too! Think about it: if you continue to breathe out and never inhale, your heart will stop beating, and you will die. Investing in self is like breathing in life-sustaining oxygen. It provides the energy for sustenance of self and for the care of others.

Society will tell us that it is impossible for a mother to obtain wealth without neglecting her family. They say she cannot balance family and financial success. Since many mothers believe this deception, they are forced to choose a life full of limitations. But, there are mothers who have been successful in all aspects of their lives. Success became achievable for them because they chose to think about possibilities instead of limitations.

## The Answer

Moms have been skipping a critical choice—an option that will allow them to stay at home (without working ten hours a day in a home office), enjoy their children, and become wealthy.

Rather than accept the choices society hands us, we can make our own. It is a laudable, achievable goal to become a stay-at-home mom who has more money and more free time than she ever had before. Motherhood, however, does not have to limit career choices. It can, instead, expand them. This book will show you how to change the way you think about motherhood, how it presents an opportunity for the creation of power and wealth without sacrificing your family's needs or any of your own. Seeking wealth does not make any woman less of a mom!

When mothers follow their passion, they will have the energy and creative ability to attract wealth, but they must be at peace with wealth in order for it to come to them. The "rich mom" will not seek wealth from a corporation or from a man. She will look into her inner abilities and find innovative ways to create wealth.

My hope is that this book will change your mind-set about the balance between financial success and mother-hood. I encourage you to allow yourself to focus your energy on creating a world of endless possibilities. Whether your passion is marketing or mothering, prosperity will come when your mind focuses on your purpose and all the potential that is inside of you. Success is in your hands.

# One

YOU ARE WHAT YOU THINK

Thoughts have power; thoughts are energy. And you can make
your world or break it by your own thinking.
—SUSAN TAYLOR

# What You Think Is What You Become

Remember the book *The Little Engine That Could*? As long as the engine said, "I think I can, I think I can," the train made progress.

Since it was first published, this book has been read to an almost endless number of young children whose parents and educators wanted them to realize the power of positive thinking.

## Positive Thoughts Produce Positive Results

The philosophy of the "Little Engine" that applied so well to the tasks of learning how to read, how to multiply numbers, and even how to tie shoes, fails somehow to transfer into the demands of adulthood—or at least into womanhood. Boys seem to pick up and practice the "I Can" message and reinforce it for their gender somehow, while girls tend to absorb messages that conflict with a can-do philosophy. Many grow up thinking "I can't."

Then they become mothers. Although they now read the same book to their children, their minds still say, "I can't." They teach their children one thing, but they believe something different.

Children are not born with minds inclined to limitations. They want to be astronauts! It is amazing what small children will do to make things happen for themselves. A mother once told me that her toddler awakened her one morning with an ice cream bar in his hand. When she went into her kitchen, she found a stool, potty-chair, and toys stacked all the way to the top of her freezer. For safety's sake, she warned her child not to do this again, but she was impressed by his creativity and determination.

Children help themselves to what they want. They don't let themselves become influenced by the opinions of others. Unfortunately, as they get older, they start listening more to what others think and often let others determine how far they can go. Before long, they put themselves in a box and tell themselves they cannot do this or have that. This way of thinking is usually set by adulthood.

Our circumstances are forged by the thoughts we allow to dominate our minds. Some people call this self-fulfilling prophecy. I have heard people say, "I knew that was going to happen." Their thoughts put them into their reality. For example, people who hate their jobs usually exhibit poor performance. Their minds are so consumed with what they do not like that it becomes difficult for them to see how they can make their jobs better. It is hard to do well at something we hate because hate takes so much mental energy that it limits abilities.

Our thoughts come from the world around us—what we read, what we see and hear, and what we experience. Did you ever notice that we are most like the people with whom we spend the most time? Their attitudes and opinions become a part of our thoughts, and we entertain those thoughts until they become part of our belief system.

Have you ever become depressed after talking to someone who is depressed? This happened because you allowed your mind to direct energy toward depression rather than happiness. Look at the people who are closest to you. There is a good chance that you are similar in voting, eating, and spending habits. You're probably even in the same tax bracket. If it's a lower one, you and your friends are stuck in mutual ideas of loss and lack.

In contrast, wealthy people focus on success, not failure. They typically surround themselves with other successful people, and they also choose not to limit their minds based on what others do or say. Wealthy people understand that their thoughts, words, behaviors, and actions create their world. The wealthy do not concentrate on past failures; they look forward to future successes. The result is an inner strength that gives them the energy and direction to pursue their passions.

Now take a closer look at the thought processes of mothers. The majority of moms will admit that their minds are focused mainly on their children. They generally focus on what they would like to do for their kids but cannot manage to do. They often forget about their own needs. Because moms become so preoccupied with providing for their children, they can come to believe that asking for more than the basics is a sign of selfishness or unwarranted discontent. Instead of being in a success mode, they tend to focus on survival and pray that their children will somehow be successful. Unfortunately these mothers will only accomplish basic survival because that is all they think about.

## What Is Your Self-Image?

The definition of self-image is one's concept of oneself or of one's role. What is the difference between millionaires and average people? The major difference is the way they think about themselves. The self-image of wealthy people is one of prosperity. Prosperity is a continuous state of success and well-being. Have you ever wondered why rich people can often go bankrupt one year and are back on top the next? Unlike most people, their thoughts are not focused on lack. Regardless of their bank account balances, they see themselves as prosperous.

The absence of a wealth mentality is the reason that ordinary people can win the lottery and then end up bankrupt two years later. The self-image of the average person is typically formed by focusing on all the negative things that have happened in her life, as well as the limiting input of others. The average person often uses past failures as an excuse to stay in her present situation.

Do you let other people shape your self-image? I did at one time. I equated my worth with my ability to be successful in the corporate world. After I left that pursuit to become a full-time mom, I lowered my own self-image by buying into the popular belief that I was no longer important because I did not work outside the home. I let other people define what my role should be.

As I spent time with other women who were stay-at-home moms, I continually heard phrases that affirmed my perceptions. We talked about what we could no longer afford. Our focus was on self-sacrifice and settling for less than the best. I saw my role as a mother undervalued, and I felt guilty if I wanted something for myself. I tried to convince myself that choosing to stay home with my children did not mean that I had to choose financial deprivation, but because I heard it so often, I began to believe it.

I believed that the role of a good mother was to put everyone else first and not complain if there was nothing left when my turn finally came. My beliefs yielded depression and fatigue. As a result, I deprived myself and my family. I gave my family emptiness because I failed to refuel myself.

Finally, a friend scolded me when she heard me say, "I can't afford that." I gave her all my lame excuses, which included, "I'm no longer working," or, "Diapers are expensive." She would not accept any of them; instead, she helped me realize the power of my own thoughts. I believed that I could neither afford anything nor deserve anything. In essence, I had a poor self-image, and my mind was continually focused on lack. When I changed my self-image and started focusing on having the things I wanted for my family and myself, the things I thought were unaffordable suddenly became obtainable. The first step was recognizing that God wants me to have the desires of my heart. When I saturated myself with stories about successful people, I realized that I did not think like they did. I decided to leave my miserable mind-set and create a millionaire mind. Instead of "I can't afford . . ." I started to ask, "How can I afford . . . ?" It finally hit me when I was helping someone put together a brochure for her business. I did not expect to get paid; I just wanted to help. She was so thankful she pulled out all the money in her wallet (about fifty bucks) and gave it to me. She said if she had more she would have given it to me. I had an epiphany right then and there. People will pay me for my business knowledge! Nothing is unaffordable to me because I have wealth-creating abilities.

Single mothers often fall into the poor self-image trap because society looks down on single parenting. They accept the current social views and are convinced that they need men to complete them. Because of this false belief, single mothers limit their success. They use being single as an excuse for failure.

If you let other people decide what you and your children deserve, they will keep you poor. I have met single mothers who spent so much time and energy trying to get child-support checks that they missed opportunities to find the wealth that was inside of them. I definitely believe that parents should honor their children by paying what they owe, but depending on child support limits the mind to a specific amount, as decided by the court. Instead of thinking, "I cannot make it without child support," the thought should be, "I can do better than child support!"

# If You Want to Change Your Circumstances, Change What You Think

I believe that every person has the ability to become wealthy, and this does not exclude mothers. However, mothers must first believe that they have the ability to create wealth and that there is nothing wrong with working toward prosperity.

Many people seem to assume that a woman's brain becomes defective when she has a baby. (I must admit that I was in a stupor for the first month, but that was from lack of sleep!) Remember the "mommy track"? After having their children, women were suddenly no longer good enough to move up in management. I find this very interesting, especially since some of the smartest women I know have never even been in the corporate culture.

# CEO? No, MomEO

The creativity of many mothers is awesome because the corporate cookie-cutter has never had the chance to taint their minds. These moms are the CEOs (MomEOs) of their homes. Their job titles include the following:

- Accountant
- Manager
- Scheduler
- Secretary
- Receptionist
- Transportation specialist
- Coach
- Educator
- Chef
- Housekeeper
- Neighborhood watch captain
- Nurse
- Community activist

- Nutritionist
- Interior decorator
- Volunteer
- Referee (especially those with several children)
- Negotiator
- Seamstress
- Buyer
- Confidante
- Lover . . . The list is far from complete.

Mothers can use their natural abilities and skills to create substantial wealth. Why just bring home the bacon? Why settle for buying bacon when you can own the pig farm? Why not provide bacon and also have time to fry it?

A woman's dream should not die when she has children. Her children should be motivation for her dream. For too long, mothers have believed the false notion that it is impossible to balance personal success and family. Mothers must get rid of "stinkin' thinkin'." "I can't afford . . ." must be eliminated from their vocabularies. They must deprogram their minds and remove negative thoughts.

If your friends speak in "I can't" terms, then they think like that, and you should probably limit your time around them until you have successfully eliminated "stinkin' thinkin'." Since thoughts form words, and words bring about existence, every thought of not enough (time, money, education, talent, etc.) must change. You can learn to feed your mind with positive information. At the end of the day, focus on the things that you did well. Mini-successes help build confidence that lead to big accomplishments. Eliminate time around negative people. You have caller ID; when that toxic person's number shows up do not answer the phone. Gradually remove those negative thinkers from your life, if possible. When you say something negative, take it back. Use the word when instead of if. Turn off the TV and read positive books. Most important, do something good for yourself. It is all right to celebrate yourself. If you wait for someone else to celebrate you (especially children), you might be waiting a very long time.

I consult with clients on how to market their careers. Often they want to change industries or focus, but they think it is impossible. I tell them that the same skills that make them successful at one company can be transferred to another company or industry. After all, CEOs and corporate executives transfer their skill sets to different companies and industries all the time.

The same skills required to run a household can be used by mothers to acquire wealth. Transferring those skills is not impossible to do. I have seen mothers type on a computer while they are talking on the phone, refereeing a dispute between siblings, and breast-feeding a baby at the same time. Now that takes skill! Mothers are typically multi-talented (especially single moms) and can successfully perform several tasks at one time. They do it because they have to survive and take care of their children. Wealthy people use this same energy, creativity, and flexibility to make themselves rich. The difference is that wealthy people believe they can prosper, while many mothers do not.

Can a mom be the next Warren Buffet, considered to be the greatest investor who ever lived? Absolutely! She can if her mind accepts the fact that she can. It is amazing that more men than women invest in the stock market, even though statistics say that women are better at it. The intuition that a woman uses to sense that her children are in trouble is the same intuition that can make her a successful investor. But if her mind is filled with negative information and fear about the stock market, she will never realize the potential wealth that is available to her through that avenue.

Mothers must develop mentalities of abundance by going beyond survival mode. Their focus must shift from welfare to wealth. It is time for mothers to revisit their dreams and start thinking about all the possibilities life presents. They must forget the past and stop dwelling on its mistakes. Their power is in the future!

# Two

## LEANNA'S STORY

Life gives us all challenges constantly. The difference
you can make is to take it all in stride, focus on the
positive, have a will to "just do it," and always strive to
reach the goals that you want in your life.
—LEANNA WELLS

## Three Strikes but Not Out

If anyone ever had reason to give up, to feel that motherhood was a near-impossible burden and one completely
at odds with prosperity, it would be Leanna.

Seven years ago, Leanna was pregnant with her third
child and confronted with a triple burden: an alcoholic husband, a dying father, and a toddler son diagnosed with cancer.

Her triumph over this incredible adversity proves the
power of will and determination. She agreed to share her story
to encourage other women to know they can do it—even if
they feel defeated!

## Battle Fatigue

"I am a very visual person and the movie *Braveheart* is something I related to while I was struggling so much. Remember
the scene when Wallace realized the person he had trusted so
much had betrayed him? He looked in his betrayer's eyes and
just lay down to die. I have felt that same way several times as
I have struggled as a single mother with mounds of stresses
beyond my control."

On February 25, 1996, Leanna was a mother of two
boys, Brandon, four-and-a-half, and Christian, two-and-a-half;

she was working full time at a call center in Oklahoma City and going to college full time.

Leanna had left her husband behind in Utah months earlier (after repeated arrests for drunk driving with the children in tow) and moved to Oklahoma City to be nearer to her father, whose heart condition was worsening.

By February 25, her father's birthday, Leanna's husband had completed a third round of rehabilitation and had joined his family in Oklahoma City after promising to remain sober for good. The four of them walked the two blocks to Leanna's parents' house, Christian complaining along the way that he was too tired to walk and had a tummy ache.

The birthday party itself was uneventful, but Leanna was under a lot of stress. In addition to Christian's complaints, Brandon was sick with an upper respiratory infection. Leanna was five months pregnant—she found out she was pregnant after leaving her husband—and the recent reconciliation wasn't going well. In the short time they'd been reunited, he'd relapsed several times. To add to this, Leanna held little hope of sharing another birthday party with her ailing dad.

## This Is What a Bruise Looks Like

Leanna took both children to the pediatrician's office the next day. While they were in the waiting room, another mother was trying to explain to her son, who had a black eye, what a bruise was and why it had created the discoloration.

"My son Christian said, 'They look like this,' and pulled his shirt and pants up to expose tons of bruises. This shocked me so much! I think the mother thought I beat him. I started to worry a lot! I had figured Brandon had an upper respiratory infection, but Christian was different. What seemed to be a stomachache turned out to be an enlarged spleen and liver."

The doctor ordered immediate blood work and said he'd have results in an hour. He said all the signs suggested that Leanna's baby boy had leukemia.

"I hadn't even heard of it before. Cancer was scary to hear. The doctor said to go home and then be up at Children's Hospital in the morning for a spinal tap. My father was always my strength. I could not count on my husband to be there at all. So my family gathered for prayer that evening. The next morning, we arrived early and the spinal was done. It came back within fifteen minutes: positive acute lymphocytic leukemia. Christian was admitted to the hospital immediately."

## Putting Life on Hold and Holding onto Life

Leanna, already having premature labor issues due to stress from her husband's drinking, dropped her college courses and took a leave of absence from work.

One month later, while Christian was still in the hospital, Leanna's father underwent open-heart surgery and died on the operating table.

"My father, my strength, was gone, only to be in my heart from that day forward. At this point I needed to be with my mother and away from my husband who caused so much more distress in an already unbelievably stressful time. My mother and I moved in together to support each other and to be there for one another."

## First One Moment, Then Another

"Right about now I was feeling very low, but I was taught early on to trust in the Lord and believe He had a plan for me. I realized that my children needed me to be strong and all I wanted to do was be strong—to focus on the positives. It could always be worse! Life's hardships can always be worse. Christian had cancer; that was a fact, but his disease was curable unlike those of other children all around us. Here I was with one son in the cancer inpatient unit and at the same time giving birth to Alec, my third son, at a different hospital. As soon as he was born we left one hospital to return to Christian at the cancer unit. I dealt with all of this by just focusing on what I needed to do from moment to moment and not dwelling on how I could do it all. Thank God for all things!"

## Starting Over, Starting Better

Soon after Alec was born, Leanna divorced her husband. Christian was released from the hospital but still required inpatient chemotherapy treatment one week per month and outpatient chemotherapy once a week. Leanna and Alec accompanied Christian while Leanna's mother assumed primary care for Brandon, taking him to kindergarten on her way to work each day.

## Not a Welfare State of Mind

Leanna was frightened, exhausted, and nearly overwhelmed, but she found the strength to look beyond her current situation and take steps to improve it. Here she was, a single mother of three boys, one seriously ill, living with her recently widowed mother and forced onto public assistance because her ex-husband spent more time in bars (or behind bars) than he did at a paying job.

Leanna accepted the welfare payments—she had no choice—but she refused to adopt a welfare mentality. Against all odds, she decided to complete the college education she'd abandoned when Christian had first become ill.

"I decided to take my last few undergrad credits as distance learning classes. I took a class on dealing with death and a few others. They helped. I did this through 1998 when

I graduated with my bachelor's degree. All the while, I was surviving on welfare to support my family and living with my mother who had lost her husband and was left nothing with which to care for herself. She worked all day and helped me with the boys every morning and every night."

Later that year, Leanna's mother won a promotion with her company and moved to Texas. Leanna shares, "Mom remarried a wonderful man whom we all love deeply, and they help me with my three boys so much."

Leanna stayed behind in Oklahoma, where she enrolled in graduate school.

"The boys and I moved onto the campus at the University of Central Oklahoma. I stayed on public assistance, took out student loans, and relied upon the support of my church to get through. I was determined to get my education because I was certain I would never get any other support from anyone other than myself, and I felt having a master's degree would help me to get a better paying job so I could finally get off welfare and support my family."

## Surviving Today, Thriving Tomorrow

Since that time, Leanna has been on her own for more than six years. Christian has been in remission from leukemia for the past four. Leanna works full-time to support her family and is on the rise at the company where she works. She is currently a recruiting manager for a major hotel chain. Although she is not yet wealthy, she has chosen a road to wealth by taking charge of her life and choosing positive instead of negative thinking.

"My goals are to continue to move up with my company and some day to buy a home for my family. I am very independent and am not needy in any way. My children play sports and we have a wonderful life. We all live in Texas now, and my mom and sweet stepdad are close by. I feel that life gives us all challenges constantly and they never stop coming. The difference you can make is to take it all in stride, focus on the positive, have a will to 'just do it,' and always strive to reach the goals that you want in your life. I am a firm believer in Christ, and I know, without a shadow of a doubt, that He carried my children and me many times when we could not walk alone.

Even though life throws us curveballs, we can still get a home run!"

# Three

## MOM EXECUTIVE OFFICER

> As those persons who despair of ever being rich make
> little account of small expenses, thinking that little added to a
> little will never make any great sum.
>
> —PLUTARCH

## What You Think Is What You Become

A successful mom and a successful chief executive officer share superiority in nearly identical skills:

⊚ NEGOTIATION

A CEO finesses lower interest rates on a loan.

A MomEO offers to do her landlord's bookkeeping in exchange for a reduction in rent.

A CEO talks a mid-level manager into taking early retirement.

A MomEO cajoles her middle child into an early bedtime.

Whose job is harder?

⊚ CRISIS MANAGEMENT

A CEO makes headlines when he meets a production schedule despite a labor strike.

A MomEO finds a last-minute baby-sitter for a sick child, so she can take her infant who just fell down the stairs into the hospital emergency room. Then she picks up the dog from the vet, packs her husband's suitcase for a business trip, and fills prescriptions for both children and the dog. After all this she makes dinner! Whose job is harder?

⊚ Financial Acumen

A CEO studies the real estate market and snatches up a dozen distressed properties he can use to expand his business.

A MomEO studies sales and clips coupons so she can stretch her grocery budget by 50 percent.

Whose job is harder?

⊚ Multitask Efficiency

A CEO is talking to a supplier in Tokyo, a buyer in Milan, and a banker in Los Angeles. At the same time he's signing letters, tipping a masseuse, and ushering his noon appointment into the office.

A MomEO interrupts a phone conversation with her son's teacher three times to answer call-waiting signals from the pediatrician, the cable company, and someone selling time-shares in Florida, while she is also making dinner, paying bills, and holding a colicky baby on her hip.

Whose job is harder?

⊚ Budgeting

A CEO who runs finances into the red has to face company shareholders and the possibility of layoffs.

A MomEO who is short of cash at the end of the month must face her family and the probability of late-fee notices and dunning phone calls.

Whose job is harder?

⊚ Bottom-Line Mentality

A CEO pays midtown Manhattan rent only if the forty-sixth floor office space is crucial to profit-making potential; otherwise, he leases a warehouse in New Jersey. He has to be hard-hearted enough to reduce payroll and to cancel holiday bonuses when sales fall behind expenses.

A MomEO pays rental premiums to keep her children in the best school district even though she could live in much nicer quarters on the other side of town. And in lean times, she has to weigh the pay-back potential of hiring a tutor for her daughter who wants to get into medical school versus hiring a voice coach for her Broadway-bound son.

Whose job is harder?

⊚ LEADERSHIP

A CEO inspires his team to work weekends, forfeit vacation time, and miss family functions in order to complete an important project on schedule.

A MomEO convinces her husband to miss *Monday Night Football*, her seventeen-year-old son to drive her five-year-old daughter to a pajama party, and her ten-year-old son to do the dishes so that she can take a night class at the local college.

Whose job is harder?

Who is more likely to be earning a seven-figure income, and who is more likely to have seven dollars in her purse? And you wonder why stay-at-home moms get depressed!

## At-Home Influence

There are two reasons mothers who choose to stay at home often feel undervalued and unappreciated:

1. Society does not honor the mother's role.
2. Moms do not honor their role.

Society will never be a force for change—it is a reaction to change. So it's up to these moms to start treating themselves with respect, to acknowledge and prove their worth. When a CEO has a good year, he rewards himself with a bonus. What does that self-sacrificing mom do when her budgetary wizardry nets a month-end surplus? She pays next month's utility bill in advance, gives in to her daughter's demands for a new pair of Nike's, or buys her husband a new golf club. What does she do for herself? Nothing—except reinforce her low self-esteem and the stereotype of the homemaker who doesn't deserve any rewards because all she really does is sit around and eat bonbons while watching soap operas and talk shows. It's bad enough that society judges people by what they do, not who they are. When women judge themselves the same way, they can't help but feel depressed.

Moms must be aware that there is a world around them that they can influence—that they are influencing! The soccer moms who made the difference in a presidential election proved that mothers had a voice and can change a nation. The "mommy-track" is not a place on the sidelines for women whose brains went comatose the moment their babies were born. It seems that women become more creative and smarter after they become mothers. Their families thrive because of it; unfortunately, many stay-at-home moms merely survive. But it doesn't have to be that way!

Women do not have to give up their dreams and visions for the sake of their children. Many mothers decide to live a life of mediocrity and take care of everyone but themselves. The mother's focus turns away from her own development toward the development of her children, leaving her in a state of stagnation while everyone else is growing.

Mothers can develop both themselves and their children. A mom who stays at home has an unparalleled opportunity to increase her influence in the school system, community, and political environment. Many mothers handle the household finances and shopping. And when it comes to influencing local businesses, there's no greater influence than money. When mothers understand the power they possess whether they work inside or outside the home, they will realize the power they have to make things happen for themselves.

Kim Danger, who launched a popular Web site for mothers, is a perfect example of an at-home mom who is influencing millions of mothers all over the country. Now she is fulfilling two dreams: the ability to stay home with her daughter and to produce residual income that has put her on the road to wealth.

## Wealth Creation

Mothers, no matter what their current job title or financial status, have the ability to create wealth. Every Mom is a MomEO. Every mom can be wealthy—without ever working outside the home. All it requires is channeling talents and energies to benefit you as well as others, rather than exhausting them for everyone's benefit except your own.

Many women are gifted shoppers; sales are irresistible to them. They have a special talent for finding bargains. This may not make sense to men, but being a good shopper is a talent. It is amazing what a mother will do to make ends meet. Moms become savvy bargain finders and sophisticated negotiators. Mothers can create a substantial income buying assets using the same techniques employed to bargain with the butcher. This is good news for the mom who is a shopaholic. She just needs to change what she buys. I recently negotiated a great deal on a car. I took my passion for being thrifty and multiplied it on a grander scale. Not only did I buy the car $15,000 below retail, but since it is predominately used for business, I can write off another $25,000 because it is a business asset. By the time I take all of the appropriate legal deductions, I end up with a $55,000 car, for approximately $7,500. This was my first time buying a car, and I did not want to do it. My husband was out of town and he pressured me into going ahead and making the decision without him. I hate the car-buying process, and I was scared. I felt like they would try to take advantage of me because I am a woman. I had to tell myself, "You are good with numbers, and you know how to negotiate." And it worked! All I did was apply the same skills that I use to run our house into buying a car. I still do not know much about cars, but I know about money. Now the money I saved can be used for investing.

And that's an important key to creating wealth: invest the money you save. Make your hard work and savvy count! If you save $100, $1,000, or $10,000, don't let that money get absorbed into the household budget. Use the money to begin your path toward wealth. Reward yourself in the same way the CEO rewards himself.

Here's another example of how you can begin small but think big. Ellen opted to breast-feed her two daughters and diaper them in cloth rather than disposable diapers. Tired of explaining to skeptical relatives about the emotional, nutritional, and environmental benefits of her decision, Ellen decided to make her point in the universal language of money. She calculated the amount of money she saved each week on formula and diapers and deposited the savings in a specially earmarked bank account. By the time her first daughter was eighteen months old, she had more than $3,000 in her milk-and-diaper fund. Not a fortune by any means, but by placing value on her choices, Ellen created value for herself.

NOTE TO MOMS:

Whether you work inside or outside the home, I suggest you take this first step toward wealth creation.

Write down all of the skills you possess. Look at the list, and you will begin to see your wealth-making ability.

Are there skills not on the list that you'd like to have?

Do what it takes to acquire them.

If you work within the corporate world, take advantage of training programs or tuition assistance opportunities. Maybe those skills won't assist you in your current job, but they almost certainly will improve your home management skills and prepare you for a life of wealth creation.

I still credit the company I first worked for after college as giving me one of the best educations in sales anyone could ever have. They taught me what college could not. I still reach back to some of the skills they taught me. Now I use them to make money for myself instead of a company.

Careerists should use their time working for someone else as stepping-stones to their own wealth. Women should not, however, trust companies to make them wealthy. Yes, that may happen for some, but the glass ceiling is real, and it is hard. For a mother, it's nearly impossible. Most of the time breaking through means breaking up a family. I am not against corporations. They provide jobs and stimulate the economy. But, I am an advocate of women having multiple sources of income. Enron is a prime example of what can happen when all of your eggs are put in one basket.

## Turn Your Seeds into a Harvest

Mothers who work outside the home should view their income as seeds that have the ability to produce wealth. True wealth is when you can stop doing whatever brings in fixed income and still live your comfortable lifestyle. Unfortunately, most people are a paycheck away from poverty.

Your fixed income can be turned into residual wealth. Moms should take advantage of what corporations have to offer through 401(k) programs. Most of them will match your contributions up to a certain percentage. Much of what you contribute is tax deductible. Now you just created another stream of income. It may not come now, but it will be available at retirement.

As a mother, you should carefully analyze every career opportunity. A promotion and a raise may not be of great value. A more important goal is to understand how to successfully manage money and build wealth. Too often, I have seen women climbing the corporate ladder, only to increase their expenses with every raise. Then when moms want to leave those jobs to start their own business or spend more time with their children, they cannot. They had simply stretched themselves too thin financially.

## More Than a Mom

Personal success does not have to be at odds with parental success. And this is not just a twenty-first century concept—there is a proverb thousands of years old that supports this concept. It is known as the story of the virtuous or noble woman. This lady was a mother who owned two businesses. Her clientele were wealthy men. Her business was so profitable she became a real estate investor. Her husband was a political figure with a lot of influence in the city. She had her own personal household staff, and her children were proud of her.

This mom's story appears in the Bible! I believe this is God's way of saying that He wants us to use all of the gifts and talents He has given us. Through these abilities, we can create wealth for ourselves—even if we are stay-at-home moms.

Perhaps, especially if we are stay-at-home moms!

# Four

## KIM'S STORY

Three years after launching Mommysavers I am making more
money than I would if I had kept working full-time.

—KIM DANGER

## From Dollars to Diapers

For most of the 1990s, Kim Danger was a full-time
corporate careerist. Married and childless, she and her
husband enjoyed the benefits of their dual income—
going out to dinner and to a movie every week, traveling,
and fixing up their house.

In October 1999, Kim became a mom and everything changed. She couldn't imagine returning to a job that
would keep her away from her daughter forty or more
hours a week. On the other hand, she and her husband
depended on her income and hadn't planned on losing it.

Kim began her transition to stay-at-home motherhood
in the same way most women do—by finding ways to
reduce expenses and live more economically. But the
knowledge, attitude, and determination that had helped
her move up the corporate ladder hadn't abandoned her,
and before long, her cost-cutting plan had turned into an
income-producing business.

### Mommysavers.com

"When our daughter Sydney was born, everything changed.
Suddenly nothing meant more to me than staying home

with her, even if it meant eating Ramen noodles and bologna sandwiches every day. Just the thought of placing her in day care brought me to tears. I just couldn't let someone else (a stranger) spend more time with my sweet baby daughter than I did. The bad news is that our family needed my income to make ends meet. So I began my strategic plan to make staying home work for us."

## Same Plan, Different Strategy

Kim and her husband didn't lose sight of their joint goal: to create wealth, but they knew they had to revise their methods if Kim's desire to stay at home with Sydney was going to fit into their goal.

They kept their immediate goal modest: to retain a small amount of Kim's income and to increase their savings. This way, they might not move as quickly as before toward their wealth-creation goal, but they would still be moving forward.

"Our plan was twofold: to make money and to save money. I needed to make a little bit of cash to help cover our monthly expenses. I also needed to save money so we could stick to our strict monthly budget for clothing, food, household expenses, etc. The saving money part would come easily for me. I've always been thrifty, and I love finding a bargain. I knew that given the extra time, I'd be able to do even better."

## Then Came the Hard Part

"The making money part of the plan was going to be the most challenging. I really wasn't interested in working retail or waitressing, and they were the only part-time jobs I could think of that would allow me to be home during the day."

# Ask For What You Want

Kim's husband, Scott, suggested she ask her employer to create the job she wanted: ten hours a week during the evenings. She expected that they'd say "no," hers had been a traditional 8:00 A.M.–5:00 P.M. environment, and they'd never made accommodations for any other employee.

"Surprisingly, they said they'd let me give it a try." And it worked out for everyone. So even before Kim founded and made a success of Mommysavers.com, she and her husband found a way to make their stay-at-home plan work. And they didn't have to eat Ramen noodles or bologna unless they wanted to. They cut back, yes, and discovered the joys of thrift stores and garage sales, but they weren't losing ground on their goals. They simply moved toward them at a slower pace.

Kim was so excited about her discovery—that it was possible to be a stay-at-home mother without draining savings accounts or plunging into poverty—she was determined to share it with other women facing similar situations. Counting pennies had become a way of life, but so was watching Sydney grow and experience new things every day.

## Shared Wisdom

"After seeing how we made it work for us, I wanted to share my experience with others. Creative budgeting, saving, and looking for new ways to make money let my husband and me achieve our dream of raising our daughter without day care. I knew that if I could do it, others could too. It didn't matter if their goal was to stay at home with their kids, to buy a new home, or to take a dream vacation. Almost anything is possible if you want it badly enough and make a strong effort to get it.

"So I set out to build a Web site with my tips and ideas. With no real computer or Web background, I had to start from square one. I taught myself how to design Web pages and began doing research for content.

"When Mommysavers was launched on Saturday, April 8, 2000, it was a simple site with about twenty pages. One year later it had more than 750 pages. Today, the site gets more than three million hits a month!

"I couldn't have done it without the great tips, advice, and ideas from the readers. Not only do I get to pass on great ideas to other moms, I get to receive them, too. What a great job this is!"

## Money Follows Passion

What began as a hobby for Kim has become a profitable enterprise. Revenue from the site—generated mostly from ads—now garners more income than her old, full-time corporate job. The love Kim had for the site shows in the dedication she brings to making it the best of its kind—and more money than she dreamed possible was the happy result.

## The Future of Mommysavers

Mommysavers.com is designed to help parents make the most of their time and money. The site includes all of the great money-saving tips and ideas that Kim has collected from real moms over the past three years.

"At Mommysavers.com we strive to share the best money-saving tips we find, and only bring you the best deals on the Web. We're not like those virtual shopping malls that include every sale and coupon code out there—we won't put anything on the site unless it is truly a good deal. Most of the bargains we tell you about are 75 percent off (or more)!

"A big part of the Mommysavers.com is our weekly newsletter. Going out to over 27,000 subscribers weekly, we include new money-saving tips, recipes, deals, and hints each week."

## Web Site Compatible

Kim's Web site venture, new to her because of its technological nuances, actually meshes well with her education and career background.

Kim has a degree in business administration with minors in home economics and Spanish. She's held jobs in creative fields such as advertising and publishing. "But nothing allows me to be more creative than operating my Web site!" When she's not working on Mommysavers.com or chasing Sydney around, Kim enjoys reading, making scrapbooks, and photography. She and her family, which also includes a dog and cat, live in Mankato, Minnesota.

## Best of Both Worlds

"Mommysavers.com has allowed me to quit my job and raise my daughter from home.

"After nearly three years of working on the Web site, I've had the pleasure of hearing personal stories from moms across the country and all over the world.

"One thing is apparent to me: money is the biggest obstacle women face when deciding whether to return to the workforce full-time after having kids or staying home. With Mommysavers.com, I want to let moms know that their choices aren't as cut-and-dried as they may think. With the Web site, I try to make mothers aware of the many options they have, whether it be generating income through a work-at-home job or making their 'job' as an at-home mom to save money through budgeting and careful shopping.

"Staying home definitely isn't what it was a generation ago. Nearly half of the at-home moms I talk to engage in some type of work that is a source of income for their families. The Web site provides me with the best of both worlds: being there to raise my daughter full-time, and experiencing of a fulfilling career and work life. Nearly three years after the site's launch, I am making more money than I would have if I had kept working full-time. What started as a hobby for me has turned into a rewarding career, both personally and financially."

# Five

KEEPING CORPORATE

> The future belongs to those who believe
> in the beauty of the dream.
> —ELEANOR ROOSEVELT

## Perks That Work

If the stay-at-home solution doesn't work for you—or if you don't want it to—there are still some mom-friendly ways to make your corporate work experience work better for you and your family.

Remember though, that although the corporate solutions will have to be approved by the corporation, the solutions themselves will have to come from you. Decide what you want, prepare your case, then ask.

Jacqueline Renaud is a single mom who has successfully negotiated more time with her child from her company. Many people equate career success to how much time you spend at the job. She has asked for things from her job that most women are afraid to ask for. Her work excellence gives her negotiating power.

To help inspire you, consider these "unheard of" benefits Jacqueline pursued and obtained from the large telecommunications company where she works as an Information Technology manager:

### Mommy Benefits

1. EXTRA VACATION TIME
   Jacqueline purchased one week of vacation in addition

to the three weeks already granted by the company. The cost for this, equivalent to one week's pay, was deducted biweekly from her paycheck.

## 2. At-Home Options

Jacqueline was given the freedom to work from home on the days her daughter was sick. The company provided a laptop, access to the LAN, and a corporate calling card. She paid for the broadband. The same option was granted on the days her daughter was out of school.

## 3. PTA Mom

Jacqueline also successfully negotiated for the ability to attend teacher conferences and other daytime school activities with the understanding that she would work later in the evening to make up for the lost time.

The key to making this work, she said, was placing her daughter in a school close to her office. This also made it possible for her to use her lunch hour to attend some school functions without missing any work time.

## 4. Overtime Solution

When Jacqueline's workload demanded staying late at the office, she had the flexibility to pick her daughter up from school and bring her back to the office.

## 5. Dual Office Arrangement

Two days every week, Jacqueline worked partly from home. On these days, she could pick up her daughter after school (she takes a late lunch hour on these days) so that her daughter could begin homework while she finished her own work.

## 6. Early Start Time

Jacqueline was allowed to begin her workday earlier than other employees. This made it possible for her to leave earlier in the day, which means her daughter spent less time in after school care.

7. Reduced Day Care Fees
Jacqueline's company paid part of the cost of day care.

8. Insurance Benefit
Jacqueline was allowed to include her daughter on her insurance policy without incurring any additional expense.

9. Book Benefit
The company where Jacqueline works has a Barnes & Noble discount. Jacqueline is permitted to use the discount to buy books for her daughter.

Jacqueline has worked at the telecommunications company for four-and-a-half years. As she continues to prove her reliability and importance to the company, she has gradually asked for and been granted increased flexibility and financial benefits that make it possible for her to grow with the company—and enjoy her daughter's growing-up years at the same time.

Ask for what you want. The worst that will happen is that you'll be in the same place you were before you asked. Women, especially mothers, are often reluctant to request special treatment or allowances for their circumstances. But try to consider it this way: If you don't ask for a flexible work schedule, you won't get it. If you ask for a flexible work schedule and don't get one, what have you lost except the few seconds it took you to ask the question? On the other hand, if you ask for a flexible work schedule—and get one—you've created an enormous, positive lifestyle change for you and your family.

You have nothing to lose and a lot to gain by seeking what you want. Approach your request for mommy benefits the same way you'd approach any other employment request (for a coveted assignment, a travel voucher, or a raise) and anticipate great results. Because great results are the kind you are most likely to achieve.

# Six

## MOMS OVER MONEY

You miss 100 percent of the shots you never take.
—WAYNE GRETZKY

## All Things Being Equal

1. Two equally gifted athletes set world running records at age twelve. One goes on to win an Olympic medal; the other becomes a fitness instructor at the local gym.

   What's the difference between them?

2. Identical twins, reared by the same parents and afforded equal education and social opportunities, inherit a trust account. At age twenty-one, they can choose to take a lump sum payment of $1 million or $50,000 a year for life. One takes the $1 million and triples it in five years through real estate investments. The other accepts $50,000 a year for the next sixty years.

   What's the difference between them?

3. Two women bake "the world's best" chocolate chip cookies. One bakes them by the dozen for family, friends, and church functions. Another launches a cookie store franchise and never bakes again.

   What's the difference between them?

1. Attitude
2. Attitude
3. Attitude

The path to excellence and independence both begin in the same location: your brain.

The athlete who wins the Olympic gold medal in the 100-meter race is not necessarily the world's fastest sprinter. Nor is it the person who had the most luck, the greatest resources, or the strongest support. What separates world-class athletes from the rest of the planet's most worthy athletes is world-class thinking. The runners, skiers, skaters, and gymnasts who bow their heads to accept a gold, silver, or bronze medal are those who first raised their heads with the highest expectations. The first step in becoming an Olympian is to think like one.

The first step toward achieving wealth is to think rich.

Consider the twins. One took $1 million out of the family trust fund. The other, over time, depleted the account by $3 million ($50,000 x 60). In a sense, the second twin was the larger benefactor—she got the bigger share of her inheritance. If there had been a fight over who would get the most of the family fortune, she won.

But it was the first twin who created a path toward wealth. By investing her $1 million, she made in five years what her sister earned in sixty. If she never made another investment and simply put the $3 million in a savings account, she could live off interest income of $150,000 a year ($3 million at a 5 percent rate-of-return) without touching the principle.

At the end of sixty years, one sister netted $3 million, all of which came from the family trust. The other, using only $1 million of the family trust, netted $12 million (the $3 million she made from real estate and the $9 million in interest income earned in sixty years).

Now, about those cookie-bakers, which one do you think was a mom—the one at her seventeenth bake sale or the one at the ribbon-cutting ceremony for her seventeenth cookie store opening? Women are born with the same recipe for wealth creation; mothers, sadly, tend to give the recipe away or stuff it into a drawer along with other sacrifices and missed opportunities.

## A Wealthy Mind

Until moms change the way they think about money, wealth will never come. Being wealthy starts first in the mind. The reason many lottery winners end up broke is because they never had a wealth mentality. The person with a wealth mentality understands that her wealth comes from her own abilities. She does not depend on other people to give it to her. Once she learns how to create wealth, she can repeat the same process even if financial devastation occurs. That is why some multimillionaires can go bankrupt and become rich again quickly. The wealthy understand the power of residual income.

The opposite of the wealth mentality is the welfare mentality. These people blame everyone but themselves for their financial situation. They leave their success in the hands of their employer. They use the economy as an excuse to do nothing. Anytime someone with a welfare mentality receives extra money, she spends it quickly. She is the one who uses her income tax returns to buy furniture instead of investing and doubling her money. She envies people with money because she feels like someone owes her something.

Although studies prove that women are better than men at investing money, they have a tendency to avoid issues and information that pertain to finance. The more mothers are educated about money, the more money they will make. I graduated at the top of my M.B.A. class and I got an A in finance, but I was never educated about money. It was an excellent school, but our educational system is not set up to teach students about money.

It is crucial that mothers invest in a financial education. Consider these statistics:

- Seventy percent of the elderly poor are women.[1]
- If you are married you are likely to live 20 percent more years than your husband will.
- Ninety percent of all women will be in charge of their own finances at some point in their lives.[2]

A friend of mine told me her dad died a millionaire and left it all to her mom. Unfortunately her mother always left the financial decision-making up to her father. Her mother died nearly penniless.

Many women put off financial planning until it is too late. Other women leave it up to their husbands, not realizing they will more than likely outlive their spouses.

It is hard to control money when you do not understand it. It is imperative that mothers inform themselves and become money-smart. The children will likely form their habits from the parents they spend the most time with, which is usually the mother. The mom's degree of financial intellect will determine her degree of financial success.

## The Money Game

The money game, until recently, has been pretty much a men-only sport. It has been easier for a woman to become a doctor or a firefighter than a Wall Street wizard. But it wasn't university admissions policies or physical requirements that kept women out of the money market. No, women have had to overcome much tougher barriers—themselves.

Finally, women are realizing that they can play the money game, and, more importantly, they can win at it! My definition of winning the money game is making the right choices so your money will work for you, instead of you working for it. If mothers are successful at playing the game, they will be able to spend more time with their families and have more money than they can spend.

## Money Game Rules

THE FIRST RULE: Know how much money you have to play with.

When people come to me for financial advice, I ask them if they have a budget. They say no, they don't need a budget because they know they do not have enough money. I then ask them how they know that without a budget. It is imperative mothers know where they stand financially in order to get ahead.

People are reluctant to draft a budget because they then become accountable to their mismanagement of money. Mothers need to learn how to do a simple budget and stick to it. If you own a computer, chances are it includes a budget program suitable to your needs. (Check out your software!) If you don't have one, you can buy one for less than $30. Do it!

THE SECOND RULE: It is not about how much you make but how much you keep.

Making money is easy. Keeping it is another talent. The average millionaire does not like to spend money. The middle class and poor try to keep up with them by spending money they do not have. Debt will always keep money away from you. It is the opposite of wealth. I believe that the only good debt is income-producing assets. An example would be a mortgage to acquire rental property with a positive monthly cash flow. Do not judge your financial success by how much money you make. Look at how much money you increase. There are people who have incomes of more than half a million dollars, and they still live from paycheck to paycheck.

If they lost their jobs they would go from well-off to poverty-stricken in less than sixty seconds.

THE THIRD RULE: Givers get.

There are certain universal principles about money that always work. Tithing is the most powerful one. Most wealthy people are tithers. A tithe is 10 percent of income. Some give it to churches, hospitals, institutions of higher learning, or various nonprofit organizations. People who consistently tithe will tell you that this provides the greatest return on their money. If your purse is always closed, no one can put anything in it. In order to play the money game, moms must be willing to give—either time, talent, or resources.

Begin small, but think big. Interest cannot accrue without an initial deposit into an interest bearing account. This holds true whether you deposit $1 or $1 million. Chances are, you don't have the $1 million today, but you probably have $1. Invest it today, commit to an investment program, and you're on your way to wealth.

It is not hard to learn the money game. I suggest reading books about money from authors like Suze Orman and getting a mentor. There are so many women out there who play the game well and have written books about it. A small investment in time could bring you a great return.

## Fear Factors

Fear is the greatest barrier to financial success. My acronym for fear is *False Evidence Appearing Real*. Most of the time fear is in the mind, fed by what we think. The mind is powerful. A simple situation can be embellished into tragedy by simple imagination. When I talk to mothers, most of their fear comes from past negative experiences. We become afraid to take the necessary steps that will allow us to prosper. We are afraid of rejection, embarrassment, or what people might say.

I think a mom's greatest fear is that if she seeks personal success, it will destroy her family. She also fears what other mothers may think about her success. Often moms assume that mothers who work outside the home or who have a successful business are bad mothers. The label of bad mother is probably a mom's worst fear.

If you are guilty of judging financially successful mothers, then you are setting yourself up for financial strife. Consciously or subconsciously, you do not want to become like them, and you will set the mental hurdles in your path to keep you from becoming wealthy. To avoid becoming a bad mother, you will make decisions that will maintain rather than improve your status quo.

Fear takes a lot of physical and mental energy. Entertaining negative thoughts paralyzes moms and prevents them from taking action. The fear of failure limits our thinking. It prevents us from coming up with those million dollar out-of-the-box ideas. What we do not realize is that successful people often have failed several times before they achieved their greatness. They may still make mistakes; the difference is they usually learn from them, then move forward. They do not dwell on past issues. The key is not to react to fearful situations, but to respond and to move on. Your emotional state controls your financial decisions. Your current financial situation is a direct result of what you allow your mind to dwell on. You cannot be wealthy without risk. As a result, the mom who allows fear to control her thinking will always sabotage her financial success.

## From Fear to Faith

Lack of faith comes from a lack of confidence. Faith is what protects you from fear and worry. The Bible describes faith as the substance of things hoped for and the evidence of things not seen. Kim, the woman who founded

Mommysavers.com, hoped to stay home with her daughter, but this contradicted the evidence that the family's household budget made it impossible.

This is where faith comes in. Kim exercised faith by building her confidence. She chose a thought process that took this leap: If I can make money outside the home, I can make it inside the home. Then she followed through and proved herself correct.

But first you have to leap. There's an Ohio man who became a millionaire selling trains. He graduated at the bottom of his high school class, and no one expected him to amount to much. So he is often asked two questions: How? and Why trains? And his answer is always the same:

"Selling is selling. I could be selling donuts. But I'd have to sell a lot more donuts than trains."

He made the leap. And he made millions.

## Fear of Money

Many times we fear money because we do not understand its purpose. As a mother on the road to wealth, you must train your mind to accept the fact that your financial success comes from smart working, exceptional planning, studying, and risk-taking. You deserve wealth, and so does your family. When you realize that your financial success is not just about you, but about your children's future, your parent's health, and a better environment for your community, the concept of creating wealth will become easier for you to embrace.

Focus on the things you do well. Major in your strengths, and minor in your weaknesses. See each day as a mini-success. Give yourself a treat when you accomplish the little things. Those small wins will provide the much-needed confidence for the big wins. Train your mind to be a filing cabinet. Put negative inputs in the back only to pull them out when necessary. Many times negative information should be deleted. Positive experiences should be the easiest to retrieve, because they are in the front of your mind.

I am teaching my children to do this. Sometimes they come home upset because a peer has criticized them. Rather than dwell on the other child's negative comments, I ask instead: "What does God say about you?" Because God only says positive things about them, I am training them to delete anything in their minds that is contrary to what God says. This allows them to keep their minds positive; it builds their confidence and allows them to make decisions out of faith instead of fear.

# Seven

## SUZANNE'S STORY

> My life's purpose is to use the gifts I was given
> as an engine moving forward, not just a vessel
> passively containing those gifts.
>
> —Suzanne Short

L ife's most important lessons may sometimes be shelved, but they are rarely forgotten. When Suzanne Short became a stay-at-home mom, she tucked away the wealth-creating lessons her father taught and put them into successful practice sixteen years later and continues to follow them today.

Suzanne grew up in Dallas during the 1940s and 1950s, the daughter of Pauline and Sam Potter, a self-made millionaire, who taught her the basic rules of a happy life.

- Character: Who We Are
- Attitude: What We Think
- Money: How to Survive and Thrive

## Poking Character with a Pin

Suzanne was just a young girl when she learned her first lesson in character. Janis, a friend of young Suzie's, was holding onto a chicken that belonged to Suzie. Janis was hurting the chicken and wouldn't put it down.

Tormented by the plight of her chicken and angry at her friend, Suzie went inside her house and found a weapon—a diaper pin. She gave Janis one more chance to put down the chicken or else she'd stick her with the pin. Janis didn't listen, and Suzie followed through on her threat.

Janis ran home crying, told her parents, and when Suzanne's father found out, he confronted her about the incident.

## Some Rules Are Golden

"Mom says you stuck Janis Sue with this big old safety pin yesterday. Is that true, Sissy?"

"Yes, Daddy. She was hurting my chicken."

"I know all about the chicken, Sissy. I want you to touch the point of this pin. You need to see how sharp this is. Go real slow and just barely touch it. Be very careful. It's pretty sharp."

Suzanne refused to touch the pin and began to cry.

"Don't you think if you got stuck with that pin that it would really, really hurt?"

"Yes, sir," Suzanne admitted.

"You can't hurt other people to solve a problem. Two wrongs never make a right. You must learn to use your head and come up with other solutions. If you are not sure that you can solve a problem without hurting someone, do nothing until you get good help to think through your options. Even when you deal with people who act badly, always ask yourself: Would I like it if someone treated me the way I am treating them? If the answer is that you wouldn't like it, then don't do it! If you live by the Golden Rule, you can't go wrong."

## Gratitude Is the Right Attitude

Suzanne's father didn't become wealthy by accepting what he had—at seventeen he was an impoverished orphan and by fifty-five, a retired millionaire—but he never forgot to be grateful for what he had, rich or poor. And this was another important lesson he taught Suzanne: there is a big difference between wanting more and being dissatisfied with what you've got. It's a subtle distinction, easily lost by anyone in the process of acquiring wealth, but it was another early childhood lesson that Suzanne said helped solidify her own quest for financial greatness.

Gratitude, her father said, is a great source of happiness. "No matter what you have, there are those with less and those with more. You had better be grateful for what you have. You have more than most!"

Suzanne took this lesson to the school yard, where she quickly found two children to envy: Billie, a pretty girl who wore pretty dresses with pretty silk bows, and Alan, a handsome boy with wavy white-blond hair and a flawless golden tan. But Alan was also crippled by polio and wore crutches under each of his perfect arms.

Thankful she didn't have polio like Alan, Suzanne also realized she had no reason to be jealous of Billie either. It didn't take a diaper-pin lecture for Suzanne to absorb the message of gratitude. Her father and mother had administered it many times before when she'd asked for a second scoop of ice cream or a new toy. And she remembered the value of gratitude throughout her adult life and financial climb: Seek more if you wish, but always be grateful for what you have.

## The Money Business

It is harder to hang on to what you have than it is to attain it in the first place. This third lesson—financial responsibility—was what Suzanne's father used to explain the fact that although he sold leather goods to earn money, his business was money.

Suzanne was in junior high and working on an English assignment that required her to write a paper about her father. When he came home from work for the weekend, she asked him what kind of business he was in.

"I'm in the money business."

Suzanne, thinking he was teasing, groaned.

"You sell leather goods, don't you? So that is your business, isn't it?"

"No, Suzie, selling is how I get our money. But I'm in the money business."

Suzanne wasn't too happy about the school assignment in the first place, and her dad just seemed to be making the assignment tougher. But she listened to his explanation: "My job is to earn enough money so that we can have food to eat, a roof over our heads, clean clothes to wear, and a safe place to sleep at night. My job isn't just to earn the money, but it is also to earn and save enough money so that you and Sammy Junior can go to college, which is something I never got to do. No, Sissy, my business is making the money and managing the money. In this day and age, making money isn't enough. You've got to learn how to keep and grow your money.

"Money is an important thing to have when times are tough. It is harder to hang onto money than it is to make money, and that in itself can be hard work. There are plenty of people waiting to take away your hard-earned money, and it is easy to get taken in. When you're in the money business, it pays to learn all you can, because a fool and a his money are soon parted."

Suzanne planned to follow her father directly into the money business. She became one of the first women at Southern Methodist University to earn an economics degree and was hired fresh out of college as a systems analyst for Republic National Bank of Dallas.

When her first child was born, Suzanne started a new career as a stay-at-home mom. Sixteen years later, to help the family add college funding, Suzanne began a career as a Realtor in Tampa, Florida, during the high-interest-rate environment of the early 1980s. Within three years, she became one of the top income-producing Realtors in Tampa and was featured in the "HOME" section of the *Tampa Tribune* for her outstanding performance.

A relocation took Suzanne and her family to Cleveland, Ohio, and Suzanne to a new career path as a stockbroker for Merrill Lynch. In her first two years, she received two bonuses for outstanding asset accumulation and became the national winner of the Merrill Lynch "The Breed Apart Campaign." She eventually returned to Texas and joined a young mortgage company, Prime Lending and became one of Prime's top originators while helping the company become the largest independent broker in Texas.

Almost nine years later, Suzanne started her own business as a full-time distributor for Excel Communications, Inc., where she rapidly promoted herself to top leadership in the first year. As an Excel rep she created and organized leadership conferences nationwide and was recognized as a top trainer and speaker.

Suzanne never forgot the lessons her father told her about happiness and how those lessons are essential to successful wealth creation. She has written many of the lessons in a book, *Wisdom Daddy Taught Me: A Path from Poverty to Prosperity*, and continues to practice them in her career, encouraging women to become more financially savvy and to take control of their destinies.

She sums up her father's lessons:

⊚ Character

Always give the other person the benefit of the doubt. Always treat the other person the way you would like to be treated. You will move more quickly to the places you want to be in life, and you will respect yourself and have the respect of others along the way.

◉ ATTITUDE

The source of happiness is found in a sense of gratitude. No matter what you have, there are those with less and those with more. Gratitude evolves or does not evolve depending on which of the two children we focus on—Billie wearing her blue-green bows or Alan leaning on his crutches.

◉ MONEY

Financial responsibility is not about the job or the size of the paycheck. Financial responsibility is about being in the business of building assets to provide for your family's needs, current and future. Managing your money to make the most of it is one of the most important skills you can learn.

From the lessons her father taught her and the ones she learned on her own, Suzanne also developed a personal mission statement, which she shares in the hope of helping other women realize their life's goals:

## Suzanne's Mission Statement

I, Suzanne Short, know, feel, and believe that my life's purpose is to use the gifts I was given as an engine moving forward, not just a vessel passively containing those gifts.

I will grow to new levels of self-fulfillment so that I have the expanded abilities to help myself and others live empowering lives without fear.

I will seek and do God's will in my life and work for the financial, spiritual, emotional, and physical welfare of not only myself, but also of my loved ones, my friends, my acquaintances, and my world.

# Eight

## PASSION—FUEL FOR YOUR VISION

I enjoy what I do and guess what? I get paid for it!
—OPRAH WINFREY

## Take Your Passion and Make It Happen

You will never become wealthy—or stay wealthy—if you are not passionate about your pursuits. Passion will give you the energy and commitment to do whatever it takes to turn your vision into fortune. If you are in a job or business "just for the money," however, it will drain you physically and emotionally, and you will never achieve great success.

Do you ever wonder why some people will hit the snooze button on their alarm clock three or four times before finally dragging themselves out of bed on a workday, and yet they will bounce out of bed at 5 A.M. on a Saturday to make a 6 A.M. tee-off time at the country club? It's usually because their job is just a job, and their hobby is their passion.

If you think it's impossible to feel as excited and energized about work as it is about leisure, then you haven't found your passion yet. And maybe you haven't spent enough time around people who have found theirs. Make an active search to find them—to read about and to meet them—and you'll be amazed at their energy levels.

People pursuing their passions can't wait to get up in the morning, and they have to drag themselves to bed at night. And it's not caffeine or fear of eviction that keeps them going. It's turbo-charged energy fueled entirely by passion. Find your passion and you have found your pathway to wealth.

## Why Do So Few People Follow Their Pathway to Wealth?

Most of us spend 80 percent of our time doing things that do not create wealth. We pursue careers that match our talents but not our desires. Or we don't even bother to consider our talents. Instead we proceed directly to the pursuit of a fast buck. A smart, qualified doctor who decided to practice medicine because her father was a doctor and because doctors make good money will never become wealthy. She'll become a doctor one patient away from poverty, a doctor who has to schedule back-to-back surgeries to keep up the mortgage payment and private school tuition—not a doctor who acquires wealth and can choose to see one patient or a hundred on any given day. She's locked into her job as much as any factory worker or waitress.

And why do you think some women choose to be strippers or escorts? Skip the theories about their unhappy childhoods and unhealthy relationships with men. They degrade themselves for the same reason some women depress themselves in more laudatory but equally dissatisfying careers: the money. Legal escorts, for instance, can earn $1,000 an hour—much more than many doctors. But you've probably never met a wealthy escort, and it's unlikely that you ever will. They hate their jobs and work as few hours as possible to get by, or they spend their income as fast—or faster—than they earn it.

Whether you are a prestigious plastic surgeon or a disrespected exotic dancer, if you are motivated by the money, you won't create wealth. Few of us are at these social extremes, but most of us work just as hard at sabotaging our progress toward wealth. Passion breaks down the barricades.

## Passion + Talent = $$$$$$$$$

Passion alone will not make you wealthy. You must focus on what you are passionate about and what you do well. For example, I am very good at doing resumes. I charged an average of seventy-five dollars for a resume. However, it was not my passion and it took up a great deal of time. After a while I realized I had bought myself an at-home job, one that took too much time away from my children. On the other hand, I am passionate about singing. I love to sing, but I am not good at it. No one will ever pay me to be a recording artist, so why should I pursue a recording contract? When your passion meets your purpose, then an explosion of wealth occurs. Look at what you're good at and what you are passionate about. There you will find your wealth.

I like to help people find their passion by taking them through a series of questions. What do you love to do? What do you do well? What have your mentors, family, and friends said you do well? Could you do those things without getting paid? What is it that you do that energizes you? Do any of these things solve problems or serve humanity? When you see a recurring theme in your answers to these questions that is your passion.

One summer I got an emergency call from the college where I formerly taught. They needed someone to teach a stock market class to fourth through eighth graders. Even though I was extremely busy, I could not say no. Money education is a part of my passion, especially when children are involved. I had so much fun, because these children had not lived long enough to let outside negative inputs hinder their faith and confidence. Because everything was last-minute, the college could not pay me the first month. I told them, "To be honest, I would do this for free." I did not care about a paycheck. Seeing children become enlightened to the value of investing was payment enough. I did get my paycheck, but I gave it all to my church.

Consider what you are doing today to earn money, and ask yourself how long you wish to continue. If your answer is until something better comes along, or until I can retire, or as soon as my daughter finishes college, then you haven't found your passion. If your answer is forever, or as long as possible, or until the day it stops being so much fun, congratulations! You've found your passion; now you're ready to use your passion to create wealth.

## Invest in Your Purpose

My purpose is to empower women to achieve financial success through money and business education. Once I realized my purpose, I had to develop it. The first thing I did was to consistently acquire information about finance and business. It only costs time to get knowledge. There are plenty of good books available to read. My home includes a miniature business and financial library. I literally have to put myself on a book budget. People often call me a walking encyclopedia, but I read, read, and read. I enjoy reading, because I am reading my passion. You would rarely catch me reading fiction.

After preparing myself with purpose, I took advantage of my past and current experiences. My children love a particular pizza place. It is loud, cheap, and the pizza is pretty good. When I go, I observe the managers and owners. Sometimes I even talk to them about the business and what makes this franchise so successful. If you work for a great company, take notice of what they do and what policies and procedures make them profitable. What is their business system? If you have a good system in place, you can prosper even with an average product. Just go to any of the top fast-food burger restaurants. Almost any mom can make a better burger, but their business system is what makes them successful.

A system is something that can be replicated. Some people make money in real estate because they get lucky or make a single good investment. People who make consistent money in real estate or become wealthy because of real estate are likely to have a system. If they buy up single-family residences as rental property, for instance, they devise a system that has proven successful. They will buy and rent a property if it meets their system requirements of market value in relation to similar properties, rental price in relation to mortgage and other monthly expenses, or even location. But they won't buy a property that doesn't meet their system requirements no matter how attractive the deal may be. If you ever wonder why some tiny towns include a McDonald's within its borders and larger towns do not, it's because the tiny town met the McDonald's system require-ments (perhaps it's close to a freeway or employment center) and the larger town, which may seem like a more attractive location, did not. If you develop a system that works, wealth creation becomes a no-brainer; the system works for you and not the other way around.

One of the best things I ever did was to find a money mentor. And I found the best. A mentor will help you get where you want to go faster and with fewer mis-takes. Many people ask me how I found my mentor. I tell them I paid for it. It was worth every penny. People who take the time to share their knowledge with you should be paid well. If a private mentor isn't in your budget, reading successful people's books can mentor you. When they write, they are sharing their life stories and the secrets to their prosperity. You can also read, for free, stories about success-ful people on the Internet. You can glean a host of useful information by reading book reviews on such sites as

Amazon.com and BarnesandNoble.com or you could check out the Web sites of wealthy entrepreneurs, motivational speakers, or their followers.

Many people, for instance, are devoted fans of Anthony Robbins and say his seminars changed their lives. If you're not ready to invest in his—or anyone's—seminar, however, that needn't stop you from taking advantage of their wisdom. People sold on Robbins are more than happy to share their stories for free.

Mark Victor Hansen, whose Chicken Soup series has sold millions of copies, is among them. One of Robbins' rules of success is to surround yourself with people you wish to emulate. If you want to be a millionaire, he says, hang out with millionaires. Hansen, as the story goes, was having no luck selling his first book and complained to Robbins that he was following the formula—he was hanging out with millionaires. Robbins told him to aim higher, to hang out with billionaires. He did, and not long after that, his book *Chicken Soup for the Soul* made the best-seller list.

Invest in the best mentoring you can afford. If your budget is still more chicken soup than caviar, begin by reading your way toward wealth.

## There's Always Room for JELL-O

The hardest part of my self-development was staying focused. I have a hard time telling people no. Broken focus took me further away from my purpose, and because I was doing things that I was not passionate about, they left me fatigued. Lack of focus will keep you trapped in your same situation. Now I evaluate everything I take on. Is it congruent with my purpose? Am I passionate about this assignment? Sometimes I get offered things that would help me financially, but realizing that it would break my focus if I accepted their requests, I turn them down. I believe that my passion will bring me prosperity.

This is admittedly scary. It's hard to turn down guaranteed money for the possibility of income. But take the risk, and you'll be amazed at the results. It's analogous to tithing. If you don't open your purse, no one can put anything inside it. Similarly, if you don't open your schedule, you can't make room for great opportunities. When you enjoy a holiday meal, you leave room for dessert, don't you? Then, be certain to leave room in your life for wealth.

## Add Vision to Your Passion

The key to achieving success is vision. Life without vision is a life that goes nowhere. Success starts with a dream. Every success story began with a dream. Dreams and visions are powered by the imagination. The imagination will always win over logic. If you imagine that you are afraid, fear will overtake you, even though there is no threat. Can you imagine yourself being rich? If you do not see yourself rich, you will never be rich. Dare to dream; it does not cost you anything.

Share your dreams wisely. One of the ways in which we lose our vision is by telling too many people—too many of the wrong people—our dreams. We share our vision with a critical parent, spouse, or neighbor. They tell us we cannot do it and we believe them. Do not tell your dreams to toxic people. There are seemingly innocent people who are dream killers, dream stealers, and dream haters. Surround yourself with people who want to help you realize your dreams.

If there's no one in your life who you know will support your vision, keep it to yourself! Then work at meeting new people, people who will say, "YES, YOU CAN!" Maybe it will be someone at your church, school, or work. It could be someone you meet at a library, at a book signing, or at a charity auction. Next time you're in a roomful of people, seek out the most positive persons in the group. It won't be hard. You'll feel the magnetic force of their energy (and you will probably see others surrounding them). Introduce yourself and ask for encouragement. Better to take the risk of finding support from a stranger than to seek the criticism you know you will get from a friend.

Too often, in moments of self-doubt, we seek out the person most likely to reinforce those doubts! A successful woman remembers the following:

"For the first forty years of my life, I compounded every negative opinion I had about myself by sharing them with my mother. What a glutton for punishment! I knew she would make me feel worse, and she did! The day I stopped calling her to confide my fears was the day I overcame them. When I was able to find just one person who said go instead of stop and can instead of can't, I changed my life forever."

Determine where you want to be five years from now, and visualize it. Write down what you want to do, and how you plan to get there. Do not worry about whether it has been done before. If you fail to plan, you are planning to fail. Create a vision board. A vision board consists of things you want to do, places you want to go, and people you would like to see. Cut out those pictures and hang the board in a place where you can see it all the time. Put on the board a picture of a home you would like to live in, or a car you'd like to have. You will soon see yourself living out your vision. Use goal cards, purpose planners, or whatever it takes to keep you focused on your purpose. A goal card is a post-card size card with one goal and three action steps. On the card you will have a deadline. On the other side of the card are small pictures and words that will motivate you to stick to your action plan. These are convenient because you can carry them with you easily. A purpose planner is a binder or notebook that holds a detailed plan. You can plan the next twenty years or twenty days of your life in your purpose planner. It combines vision board pictures and words as well as your strategic plans to accomplish your vision. Each project can be one to three pages. In this book you can put book ideas with titles, new product concepts, and research on a business you would like to start. It is your personal dream book. You can also instill goal setting in your children by having them do vision boards.

## What You See Is What You Get

The old saying of seeing the glass half empty or half full is true. If you see a horrible economy, your life will be a victim of a horrible economy. If you see an economic opportunity, then you will find ways to prosper regardless of any economic situation. It is amazing to me that the market can be down, but there are still companies reaching an all-time high. I talk to unemployed people, and they always say there are no jobs. Because that is what they believe, they choose to stay on unemployment and do not do what it takes to find a job. They spend most of their time listening to newscasters tell them how high the unemployment rate is. Instead of looking at an unemployment rate of 6 percent, why don't they see an employment rate of 94 percent? There are many wealthy people who are completely unaware of the unemployment rate; it's not a factor for them because they don't allow it to become one.

For too long, mothers have seen themselves as second-class citizens. If that is the way you see yourself, then that is how the world will treat you. Why not see yourself as innovative and intelligent? See yourself as a money magnet. It is okay to see yourself driving a luxury car. If you play the money game right, you can have that car for less than the price of an average minivan. Because so many people choose to believe we live in a world of scarcity, it is important to surround yourself with visions of abundance. When you see abundance, you will get abundance.

Here's how to P. A. V. E. your way to wealth:
P IS FOR PASSION.

It will fuel your journey.
A IS FOR ABILITY.

It is your ticket to greatness.
V IS FOR VISION.

It will guide you and keep you focused.
E IS FOR EXPECTATIONS.

They will bring you and wealth together.

# Nine

## RENÉE'S STORY

Your passion will give you the energy to
accomplish a dream, but your priorities determine
their stability and longevity.

—RENÉE HORNBUCKLE

## From Boardroom to Bored

Renée Hornbuckle is a gifted motivational speaker who has walked, as well as talked, her way from corporate life to becoming a stay-at-home mother to entrepreneur. Renée is devoted to helping other women find their own paths.

She also knows how difficult those transitions can be and empathizes with women who have found themselves uncertain, ungrounded, and unhappy when motherhood turned their lives upside down.

"Having gone through several transitions in my life, I am convinced that women can maximize their lives if they recognize the seasons that they are in.

"Upon leaving corporate America, I faced a personal crisis. I was a corporate executive who seemingly had it all together. I had a great husband, two young children, and a promotion on the job. Life seemed manageable. Then it happened. My husband asked me to leave corporate America and assist him in his dream. So, I came off 'the job' and my downward spiral began.

"Who was I? What was I going to do now? There were not any awards given for being a mom—no promotions, no accolades—nothing. It seemed as if my rewards were laundry, diapers, crying children, and never-ending mundane work. I began to lose sight of myself. I became depressed."

# You Can Take the Woman Out of the Corporate World, but . . .

"One day in my depression, I caught a glimpse of the corporate woman I used to be. I saw myself giving presentations and inspiring my team to get the job done. It dawned on me, 'That person still exists!' All I had to do was to discover her again. So, I went on a personal journey to determine who I was and what I wanted to do. I knew I had to do something. I needed a business that would help others. It then became my personal goal to assist other women in achieving their goals."

## Starting Small, Thinking Big

"I began to speak to small groups of women. Before long, that small nucleus grew to several hundred. In trying to reach more women, I made the determination that I needed to expand my influence by writing books. I founded Women of Influence (W.O.I.) in 1996."

Women of Influence, Inc., is a ministry committed to the personal development of women worldwide. Through her speeches, conferences, and books, Renée challenges and inspires women everywhere to maximize their potential and realize their God-appointed destiny. By equipping women through her ministry, Renée causes ordinary women to transform into women of influence, distinction, and worth.

Renée has been a featured guest on the award winning show *Good Morning Texas* to discuss her role as mentor to the wives of NFL players. She also has cohosted *Solutions* shown on Daystar Network Television and has appeared on the Trinity Broadcasting Network as well.

Renée's ministry is dedicated to training others, especially women, in practical life skills and character building so that they can live enriched lives. Through biblical instruction and personal experience, she is able and qualified to communicate the principles of successful living with conviction.

Best known for her uncompromising style, Renée hosts the annual Women of Influence Personal Development Conference and is the author of *If It Pleases the King,* a practical guide to hospitality; *Destined For Greatness,* a developmental program aimed toward teaching entrepreneurial, education, moral, and social skills to young people; *The Power of Healthy Esteem;* and *The Power of Passion.*

Renée hosts a variety of seminars designed to empower women with practical skills for success including monthly seminars that cater to women who stay at home, as well as those who are employed in power positions in corporate America. Renée has added corporate training and life coaching to her schedule. On top of all that, she built a transitional home for women and is opening a restaurant.

Additionally, Renée assists her husband, Bishop Terry Hornbuckle, in overseeing Agape Christian Fellowship—one of the nation's fastest growing churches. Together they manage the South Central Region churches affiliated with Kingdom Dominion Network and the Agape Fellowship of Ministries.

## Bottom Line Looks Fine

"W.O.I. continues to assist and encourage women from all walks of life. As a motivational speaker, entrepreneur, and author, I have exceeded my income several times over what I would have done in corporate America. Not only do I enjoy what I do, but I am financially secure as a result."

Renée holds a bachelor's degree in business administration and a master's degree in biblical studies. Above all, she enjoys ministering to her husband and their three children, Matthew, Rachel, and Jordan.

"In the midst of all this activity, I am a wife and mother. The road to success is often long and hard, but with determination, focus, and a proper priority structure, any dream is achievable. Every now and then, I have to evaluate where I am, what I need to eliminate or add into my life, and where I would like to go in the future. My main determining factor is 'How will this affect my family?'"

Your passion will give you the energy to accomplish a dream, but your priorities determine their stability and longevity.

# Ten

## FROM PASSION TO PROSPERITY

Passion doesn't remove obstacles, but it does
ignite our determination to overcome them. We can
nurture our passion so that it becomes the catalyst
that helps us realize our ambitions.

—Marion Luna Brem

## Unstoppable Passion

I identified the one thing that provided me
with the greatest joy—encouraging others.

— Cynthia Kersey

Giving up a lucrative salary as a sales executive for a communications company, Cynthia started a five-year journey to identify her true passion. Cynthia discovered that encouraging others was her unique calling. After cashing in her family's life savings, Cynthia spent eighteen months interviewing hundreds of America's greatest achievers. She discovered specific behaviors and strategies that enabled ordinary people to achieve extraordinary success. Cynthia put these inspirational stories in a book called *Unstoppable*.

As an author, speaker, and mother, Cynthia touches thousands of people's hearts by living her true passion: sharing the stories of unstoppable people. Cynthia motivates her audiences by chronicling people who have demonstrated what is possible for anyone with a commitment to achieve their true heart's desire.

# Prosperity Passion

In everyone's life there are probably three to four major passions. Not all of these will be their prosperity passion. For example, I know someone who has a passion to feed the homeless. It is an honorable passion, but he needs money to feed the homeless. He must use his prosperity passion to bring him the much-needed wealth to expand his purpose.

Mothers must find their prosperity passion. I teach moms a four-step process. This enables them to focus on one specific area that will bring them wealth. From this wealth they will be able to support their other passions.

### ⊚ Step One

What do you love to do? You must list the activities that give you pleasure and satisfaction. These activities will excite you. They may be a hobby or something you always wanted to do. These activities will energize you. You wake early and look forward to doing these pursuits. You will stay up late and do them when you are tired.

### ⊚ Step Two

From this list, which ones are you really good at? These will be activities in which you excel. Do people compliment you when you do these things? Have your mentors recognized this talent? This passion should be a strength area for you. Remember my passion for singing? It would not make it past this step, so I have to go back to step one.

There should be a history of success with this passion.

### ⊚ Step Three

Your list will get smaller by step three. Is the item congruent with your purpose or calling? Is this what God wants you to do? Would you do this activity for free if you were wealthy? Do you feel like you could make a difference with this passion?

## ◉ STEP FOUR

This is the step that will allow your passion to bring you wealth. In order for passion to turn into money, it must answer yes to one of three questions.

1. Does it serve?
2. Does it solve?
3. Does it seduce?

If it does not fit in one of these categories, then go back to step one.

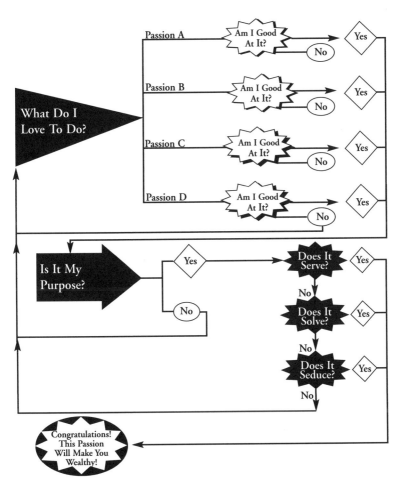

# Serving Up Fun for Families

I knew I wanted to help parents understand
the importance of playing with their children
and give them high-quality toys that would be
educational as well as entertaining.
—LANE NEMETH

As founder, president, and CEO of Discovery Toys, Inc., and mother, Lane Nemeth had a passion to serve families by making educational toys available to the public. With $5,000 in her pocket, she started Discovery Toys from her garage. From her passion, Nemeth created wealth and opportunities for both her family and mothers with young children who created their own wealth from home businesses.

Nemeth's commitment and entrepreneurial spirit has thrust Discovery Toys to great success "I use my mothering skills in my business everyday." Lane Nemeth has received numerous business awards and she is a featured speaker at national child development, business, and leadership seminars.

When your passion serves a specific population of people, they are willing to pay you for it because they have a need that is not being met. An unmet need translates into an opportunity for mothers who want to create wealth.

# Solving the Problem of Financial Illiteracy

I love my children and want to ensure they get the best
education possible! Traditional schooling, while very
important, is no longer enough. We all need to
understand money and how it works.
—SHARON LECHTER

Mother, CPA, and coauthor of the Rich Dad, Poor Dad series of books and CEO of the Rich Dad Organization,

Sharon Lechter uses her passion for education to solve a significant problem. Recognizing a gap as her children went through the educational system, Lechter created a number of financial educational tools to give people what they need to survive and flourish in our quick-paced global and high-tech world. A pioneer in her own right, Lechter has not only used her passion to create wealth for herself, but she is educating other people to do the same.

People who make the most money are problem solvers. The more difficult or widespread the problem, the more money you will make. Mothers have unique problem-solving skills. They are constantly in problem-solving mode. Does your passion and talent solve a problem? Then you have wealth waiting for you.

## Seducing America One Cookie at a Time

You've got to love what you do. I believe that when
you love what you do, you will be great at it. You
will be obvious. Other people will see that,
and it will cause you to be promoted.
—DEBBI FIELDS

Business owner, author, and mother Debbi Fields rules a multimillion-dollar cookie empire. Her passion had been evident since she was a child. She loved baking cookies and sharing cookies and was lovingly known as the "cookie kid." When it came time for a career, there was no question about what she would do. "I found lots and lots of obstacles. As you are venturing out into the world and you love what you do, and you are passionate about it, you have to believe in your heart that no is an unacceptable answer. It will give you the courage to keep knocking on doors."

The power of seduction is great. Those passions that entertain and give enjoyment are in this category. The moms whose passions fall in the creative arts categories would fit here. Think about it. Even when the economy is at an all-time low, movie and music sales are still high. People are still waiting in line at restaurants. And we all know Krispy Kreme is not hurting.

## It Can Happen for You

Lane Nemeth, Sharon Lechter, and Debbi Fields are all millionaire moms. They love their children. They had a dream and followed it. Yes, they all had obstacles, but since it was their passion, they persevered. How does a young housewife with no formal education become a top businessperson? Debbi Fields comments, "Just like the little train that could, that attitude will get you further and further. The moment you say you can't, you are defeated. You can never use the word can't. You've got to believe. You have to have the right attitude. More importantly, you just don't give up."

## Think About It!

Business ownership has been one of the most effective ways of improving women's economic well-being.[3] Women-headed households with a business had an average income level of more than two and a half times those without a business, and six times their net worth in 1998.[4] Women-owned companies are growing three times faster than all U.S. businesses.[5]

# Eleven

## ELLEN'S STORY

When the goal is yours – and yours alone – nothing
and no one can keep you from achieving it.
—ELLEN SINGER

## Wiped Out but Not Erased

At age twenty-three, without ever working more than fifteen hours a week, Ellen Singer had made enough money to pay cash for a new car, put a down payment on a house, and take her mother to Disney World.

At age forty-three, after regularly working fifteen-hour days, she was living in an eight-year-old car with two daughters, plus two dogs, and trying to figure out how to feed them all on $7.53—all the money she had to her name.

Today, sixteen months later, by applying the wealth-creation wisdom of her youth, she's recovering financially and enjoying life as an at-home entrepreneur who can help her daughter with geometry homework or bake a pie midday without fear of her boss's reaction—because she's the boss.

## $1 or $1 Million— What's the Difference?

"I was always good at making money. I had the talent and determination to work my way to the top of whatever environment I was in, but my career destiny was always shaped by factors beyond my control—whether a company folded, a mentor moved, or university enrollment dropped.

"I took it in stride knowing I could always find another job, could always make another dollar, and, in fact, made more than $1 million. But the money and my ability to remain in the workplace ran out at the same time. And I couldn't see a way out of the mess."

## Unusual Circumstances, Usual Reasons

Ellen's history includes more drama than most—she and her children were forced into hiding after a psychopathic ex-husband stalked them for five years and hired a hit man to kill them—but the elements of acceding control to a husband, an employer, or to a friend are common to many women, particularly mothers.

## The Price of Evil

"When I was in college, I got an unexpected student loan. I was going to just return it but took a look at the low interest rates being charged and decided to hold onto it. Then I decided to invest it and turned $2,000 into $30,000 in less than a year, then tucked the whole thing away in a long-term account. It was more than luck; I paid serious attention to the market, never got too greedy and got out while the investment was still growing. I never told anyone I was doing this, just got it in my head that I could and would do this and followed through.

"After I got married, though, I lost that sense of mission—and much of myself. Although I was the major provider for the first half of my marriage, from day one I gave up control of the finances to my husband. I worked ten hours a day; he worked five. I saved; he spent. Eventually, it didn't matter how much I made, I never saw any of it, so the value of money in my life evaporated.

"When the marriage turned bad—cruelly abusive—and I fled with my daughters, I was prepared to spend my half of our assets (about $250,000) to obtain a divorce and to protect my daughters. But I wasn't prepared for a five-year battle that would end up costing more than $500,000 and force me to give up my career, my home, my friends, and my family."

## Kill Him or Disappear

Ellen spent every penny she had to get a divorce—she gave her lawyer the family auto to settle his bill—but was quickly earning high wages as a New York-based writer. She was on her way, she believed, to fame and fortune, her unhappy past behind her. But her ex-husband had other plans, stalking her relentlessly via cyberspace and with the help of private detectives, ultimately hiring a hit man.

Ellen tried every legal avenue to keep her ex at bay, but when the New York police told her there was nothing they could do about the hit man—until it was too late—she was left with two choices: kill her ex-husband or disappear with her children.

Disappearing was legal. She had full custody, and he had no visitation rights. She and her daughters walked out of the Upper West Side apartment one morning, saying their usual good-byes to the concierge and the homeless men who relied on them for $1 a day. They followed their normal route to school but went inside one door and out another, traveling by taxi, subway, train, plane, bus, boat, and auto to a place where they knew and were known by no one.

## New Chapter, Same Refrain

"I was broke—again—but confident I could work my money-making magic one more time. I had a master's degree, an impressive job history, and recommendations from household names in the publishing and business worlds. The problem was I couldn't safely apply for any job that used my marketable skills or A-list contacts—it would leave a trail my ex could follow. Suddenly I felt like I'd done more than given up my identity. I'd given up my existence."

Ellen's reaction to being stripped of her credentials was to think like a person who didn't have any.

"Success was no longer a concept to me; wealth seemed impossible. I developed a day-to-day mentality, eking out a living training dogs and selling handmade crafts. We were poor, but we were safe. It was a trade-off I was more than willing to make, but working at menial tasks didn't suit me. I felt useless, powerless, and kept slipping further behind until one day I was forced to move out of my apartment (the land-lord sold the building), and we had nowhere to go."

## Would You Hire This Woman?

Ellen had allowed her circumstances to alter her viewpoint. She had started to think of herself as poor and uneducated and couldn't imagine anyone wanting to hire her even if she could safely apply for a job. Then she had a revelation: "I could hire myself! Maybe I had lost my name and my credentials, but I hadn't lost the talent that went with them. Somehow I could write my way out of my financial predicament and into a financial success."

The change in attitude changed everything. Ellen wrote a book about her experience that was published by Harper Collins and is being produced by Hearst Entertainment as a movie-of-the-week. She took out an ad on the business Web site, Elance.com, a source for freelance jobs, and met her one-year goal of becoming Elance's top-producing writer. Even more importantly, she's started thinking like a wealth creator again.

"I was so broke it took me three months to scrape up the $50 to subscribe to Elance. But I quickly saw it as a way to do more than just earn an income. I had a chance to profit from other people's success as well. I could do more than just ghostwrite other people's work. I could help them get published—by now I knew how—and if I owned just a tiny portion of each project, I'd earn money far beyond the original compensation. If I made 5 percent of a book that sold for $10,000, I made $500 that I didn't have to sit at my computer earning. If the same book sold for $100,000, I made $5,000. I don't own pieces of all the projects I've worked on in the past year, but I own half of some of them, and I've helped more than a few clients land important contracts."

## Destiny: Fame and Fortune

"Two of my clients happen to be spiritual advisors, and both say I'm destined to be a millionaire. I believe them, and the reason is that I've started thinking like a millionaire. I've begun to see success ahead rather than failure behind. I took charge of my goal—to be a full-time writer working for myself—and the passion and commitment that followed have propelled me to new heights. It hasn't been easy. I routinely work sixteen-hour days and am hard hit when a deadbeat client disappears with money I've earmarked for rent. But I love working for myself and am dedicated to making myself successful. Because the goal is mine, I know that nothing and no one will stop me from achieving it.

"That's the message I've tried to share with my daughters—now in their teen years—and would like to pass onto other women: you can and will achieve any goal you set as long as it's a goal you've chosen yourself. Aim to become a doctor to please your parents, and you may or may not get through medical school. Aspire to be an astronaut because space exploration is your passion, and you'll find a way to blast off!"

# Twelve

## SPEAK YOUR FUTURE

Speak to your future you, instead of your past you.
—TERRY HORNBUCKLE

## Your Words Create Your World

Your thoughts form the words that create your circumstances.

Find someone who always has something negative to say, and you will find a person who can never seem to get ahead. Their words hold them back. Believe that you will fail, and you will find a way to make it happen. Most of us accept this as a basic truth. We have more trouble accepting the inverse: Believe that you will succeed, and you will do whatever it takes to succeed. The latter statement is just as true as the former statement.

Words are powerful. The earth was created by words. You have power to create your future. Stop saying you can't afford it! You cannot afford to say that any more.

When Ellen gave up her income, her home, and all of her belongings to go into hiding from a husband who was stalking her, she had less money than at any other time in her adult life. She moved to one of the wealthiest areas in North America to ensure that her daughters would envision a future of prosperity and potential. This was not a practical decision (she could have stretched her limited dollars five times further in another area), but it was a decision borne of vision. No matter how poor her family was, they would understand and feel comfortable in a world of riches.

One of my greatest life lessons growing up was eliminating the phrase "I can't." My parents would not allow us to say it. In our house, it was almost like cursing. As children, that built our confidence. Neither one of my parents were high school graduates. There were six of us. My mother stayed at home, and my father worked. We were pretty much lower middle class. Because of the positive conditioning of my parents, all of us have college degrees, and more than half of us have a post-graduate degree. My parents had not gone to college, but they told us we could. Even my mom went to college after the age of fifty and received a degree.

## Are Your Words Limiting Your Success?

- ◉ We have only one income.
- ◉ My children are too young.
- ◉ I do not know anything.
- ◉ I do not have time.

We believe what we say, and that determines the decisions we make. Your past decisions are what created your current situation. The notion of sticks and stones is wrong. Words do hurt, but words can also heal.

I challenge you to listen to what you say. Each time you say negative things about yourself or situation, you limit your success. I often hear moms say they do not need any more money. They believe that wanting more money is selfish. I say I need more money because there are homeless children, battered women, smart kids who cannot afford college, and diseases that need a cure. Mothers actually think they are being selfless by saying they do not want wealth. The only selfish stance is one in which you create only enough money for your family and let everyone else fend for themselves.

There is power in our positive confessions. When people ask me if I am a millionaire, I tell them: "Yes, in my mind I am. I am just waiting for the physical manifestations in my bank account." They laugh. I have no doubt that we will be wealthy. I tell myself everyday that I attract abundance, and it is God's will for me to prosper. Why do people ask me if I am a millionaire? Because I talk (and think) like one!

## You Have Not Because You Ask Not

There is an old saying that, "Life and death are in the tongue." You can speak life into your finances. As mothers, we limit ourselves because we ask very little from life. Asking is out of our comfort zone as women. We feel that this is an aggressive male characteristic. Our hesitancy in asking keeps us out of the money game. Many times we do not ask because we are afraid of getting no as a response. And you will get no, but that does not mean you should give up. Successful authors are often turned down many times before they get a book published. Those books often become best-sellers. If they had quit trying, their lives would have stayed the same.

If you look at children, they do not have a problem asking for what they want. My children will not accept no the first time. My goal is to get them to never fear asking but to understand that I mean what I say. Children who ask for the same thing several times over really believe that they will get what they ask for. And many times that is true. If you want to truly be financially successful, you must believe you will get what you ask for. You may not get it right away, but eventually, it will come to you.

Jacqueline's story is a great example of what mothers can get from the corporate world if they have the courage to ask.

When I used to help people with their interview techniques, I always told them to make sure they asked for the job. Many people have missed out on jobs and promotions because they did not ask for them. If you are a highly qualified person, it is hard for employers to tell you no. You are asking them to make a commitment: If you like my skills, hire me. There is nothing to lose from asking. If no is the answer, then you are still right where you started.

## As a Mom Thinketh

The journey to financial success takes a "just do it" approach. Write down your goals and visit them everyday. Ask for what you need to make it happen for you. As a mom, you can barter your time, talent, and resources. Tell yourself that someone will give you what you need. If you never start the business, how do you know if it will work? God gives everyone the ability to create wealth. There are million-dollar ideas God has circulating in the universe. He is waiting for someone to grab one and do something with it.

I always tell moms to develop a mommy-network. One mother I knew became a successful author because her friends kept her children once a week while she wrote. I started Mom Executive Officers (MomEOs) because I wanted mothers to come together to learn about business and finance. I also wanted to have a place where mothers could barter, network, and support each other's dreams. MomEOs is a safe place for mothers to say, "I love my family, but I want more." The great thing about MomEOs is that women who are not moms are joining. They know there is more available for them, and they want help in achieving their purpose. All women can join. The rule is that members must speak positive words, and must not limit anyone's dream. I give a disclaimer to all who inquire: If you think wealth is wicked, then this is not the organization for you. For more information about MomEOs you can go to www.momeos.com.

Think outside of the box. Go beyond what is the norm as dictated by others. A mom can employ the same creativity she uses to get her child to sleep or to eat green vegetables, and she can apply it to her quest to become successful. Mothers who saw an unmet need created many of the items we use for our children today, and they became wealthy during the process.

Regrettably, the majority of people will not become wealthy because they are satisfied with mediocrity. They do not see themselves in a nice home, driving a fine car, or having more time to spend with their family. They leave their future in the hands of the government or their employer. Most people will allow the news or the economy to dictate their prosperity. The wealthy person will always find a way to be successful no matter who is in political office or where the stock market is. The welfare mentality person will say it does not take all that much to be happy, and they are right. But, there is nothing wrong with wanting more out of life. I realized that being wealthy was bigger than I was. People with a prosperous mentality do it for more than themselves. Our hospitals, schools, and social services are successful because someone shared their wealth in order to help others.

You can be the next rich mom! I made a few adjustments to a famous poem to empower mothers.

> If you think you are beaten, you are.
> If you think you dare not, you don't.
> If you like to win, but you think you can't,
> It is almost certain you won't.
>
> If you think you'll lose, you're lost,
> For out in the world we find,
> Success begins with a mother's will.
> It's all in the state of mind.
>
> If you think you are outclassed, you are.
> You've got to think high to rise.
> You've got to be sure of yourself before
> You can ever win a prize.
>
> Life's battles don't always go
> To the stronger or faster man.
> But sooner or later the mom who wins
> Is the mother WHO THINKS SHE CAN!

**You can be the next rich mom!**

# APPENDIXES

# APPENDIX A

## What Is MomEOs?

Mom Executive Officers (MomEOs) was created by President and Founder Del-Metri Williams. The vision of MomEOs is to empower mothers to financial wealth through entrepreneurship, investments, and financial literacy.

MomEOs is a networking organization for mothers to increase their financial acumen and develop wealth building strategies. Mothers will be able to assist one another through the mutual exchange of contacts, referrals, and resources.

Do you have a million dollar idea? Mothers can use their natural skills and abilities to create substantial wealth. MomEOs will give you the networking and mentorship opportunities that you need to be successful.

Every seminar and meeting is catered toward mothers. Business and finance is taught in a light, humorous, and dynamic way. Mothers will learn how to balance success and family while actualizing personal financial goals.

Are you the next rich mom? You can be. MomEOs will give you the support and encouragement you need to make your dreams come true!

For more information go to www.momeos.com and sign up for a free money report.

# APPENDIX B

## Share the Wealth

For every successful woman you hear about there are many others that need help. Author Del-Metri Williams has chosen Rachel's House as her charity of choice.

Rachel's House will offer transitional housing and training services for women and their children who are experiencing financial difficulty due to loss of employment, a recent divorce, domestic abuse, or domestic upheaval. Rachel's House will address these issues through training designed to nurture the 1) mind, 2) body, 3) spirit, and 4) self. They will train women in work etiquette, interviewing skills, self-esteem, and emotional stability assuring better lives for them and their children.

Working women with children make up a silent and rapidly growing population whose needs fail to be met by the church or government. Homeless shelters do not address the needs of the workingwoman, and while there are various facilities that assist battered women or those recovering from chemical dependency, there are limited resources for women who find themselves struggling under the financial strains of divorce, layoff, bankruptcy, or other devastating events.

Rachel's House is a nonprofit organization and will be open June 2003. A portion of the proceeds from every *As a Mom Thinketh* book sold will go to help fund Rachel's House. Join us as we make a difference by providing a safe, positive environment for women in need. For additional information regarding Rachel's House visit www.womenofinfluenceonline.com.

# APPENDIX C

## Recommended Reading
### FOR INVESTING IN YOUR FINANCIAL FUTURE

*The One Minute Millionaire,* Mark Victor Hansen and
Robert Allen

*Rich Dad, Poor Dad,* Robert T. Kiyosaki and Sharon L. Lechter

*Multiple Streams of Income,* Robert G. Allen

*The Courage to Be Rich,* Suze Orman

*Smart Women Finish Rich,* David Bach

*The Complete Idiot's Guide to Investing for Women,* Jennifer
Bayse Sander, Anne Boutin, and Jim Brown

*Mompreneurs,* Ellen H. Parlapiano and Patricia Cobe

*Everywoman's Money™: Financial Freedom,* Dee Lee

*Think and Grow Rich,* Napolean Hill

# ENDNOTES

1. Business Week Online, January 31, 2001

2. U.S. Department of the Census, 2001

3. U.S. Small Business Administration Office of Advocacy Report, *Women in Business,* 2001

4. Ibid.

5. *Working Woman,* June 2001

# About the Author

With over fifteen years of experience in sales, marketing, and consulting, Del-Metri Williams has a broad understanding of the business and financial worlds. After leaving a corporate career, she began helping small-business owners market their products and services while teaching a business class at Tarrant County College. She quickly discovered that many of the business owners were very talented but lacked financial acumen. Soon her consulting became financial education.

Although she assists a variety of people, her passion is focused on women who want to change their lives and start living their dreams. She currently gives business and wealth-building presentations targeted specifically toward mothers from all walks of life. She is the president and founder of MomEOs (Mom Executive Officers), which was created to empower mothers towards wealth through entrepreneurship, investments, and financial literacy.

Ms. Williams holds an M.B.A. in marketing and management, as well as a B.S. in business administration. She is married and is the mother of two children.

Bring Del-Metri Williams to your next event to enlighten your group in a style that is dynamic, humorous, and uplifting; she challenges people to change the way they think about money, and they leave her presentations wanting more.

E-mail: info@momthink.com